JUL - - 1999

LIJ

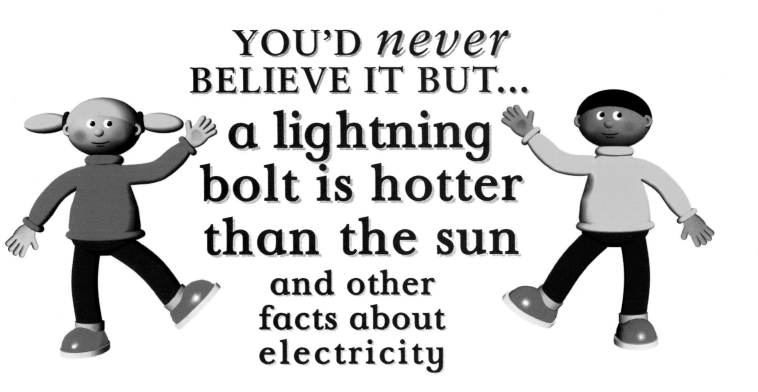

YOU'D *never* BELIEVE IT BUT...

a lightning bolt is hotter than the sun

and other facts about electricity

© Aladdin Books Ltd 1998

Designed and produced by
Aladdin Books Ltd
28 Percy Street
London W1P 0LD

First published in the United States
in 1998 by
Copper Beech Books,
an imprint of
The Millbrook Press
2 Old New Milford Road
Brookfield, Connecticut 06804

Designed by
David West Children's Book Design
Designer
Flick Killerby
Computer illustrations
Stephen Sweet (Simon Girling & Associates)
Picture Research
Brooks Krikler Research
Project Editor
Sally Hewitt
Editor
Jon Richards

Printed in Belgium

Library of Congress Cataloging-in-Publication Data
Taylor, Helen (Helen Suzanne), 1963-
A lightning bolt is hotter than the sun and other facts about electricity / by
Helen Taylor ; illustrated by Stephen Sweet.
p. cm. — (You'd never believe it but—)
Includes index.
Summary: An introduction to electricity, discussing static
electricity, turbines, batteries, magnetism, and other uses and
safety aspects of this power source.
ISBN 0-7613-0862-8 (lib. bdg.)
1. Electricity—Miscellanea—Juvenile literature.[1. Electricity.]
I. Sweet, Stephen, 1965- ill. II. Title. III. Series.
QC561.T39 1998   98-28786
537—dc21   CIP AC
5 4 3 2 1

YOU'D *never* BELIEVE IT BUT...

a lightning bolt is hotter than the sun

and other facts about

electricity

Helen Taylor

C O P P E R   B E E C H   B O O K S
B R O O K F I E L D ,   C O N N E C T I C U T

Contents

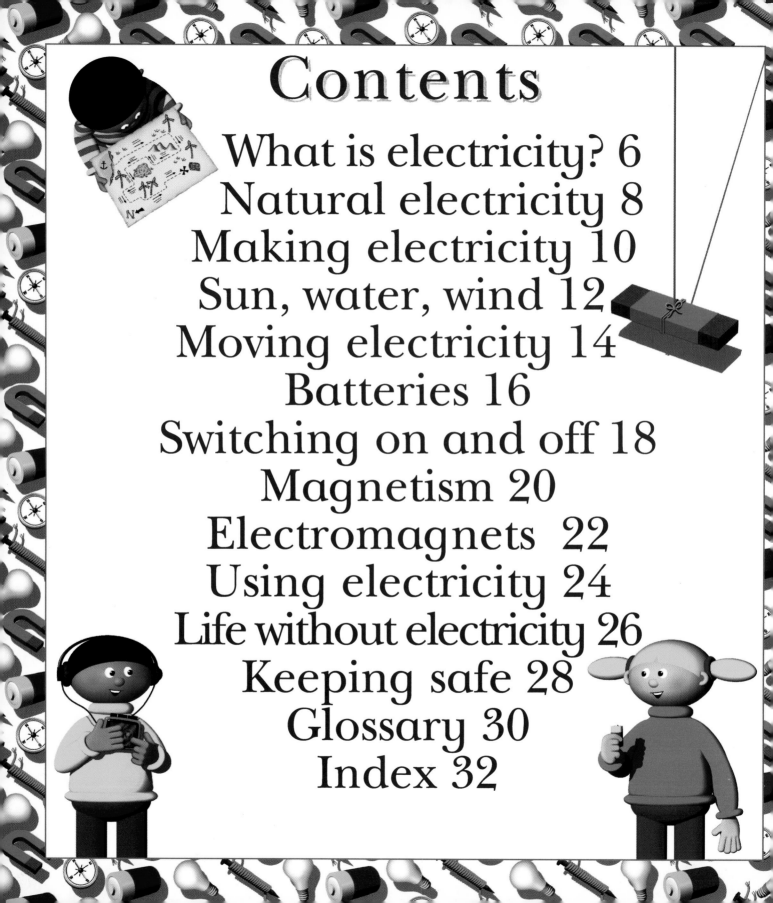

Introduction

Electricity flows all the time through cables buried under our feet or hanging over our heads. These cables carry it into our houses, schools, and workplaces, keeping them warm and bright, and making machinery work.

Join Jack and Jo as they learn all about electricity, including how it can light a bulb, how it can pick up objects, and why it flows through our bodies.

FUN PROJECTS
Wherever you see this sign, it means there is a fun project that you can do. Each project helps you to understand the subject.

WARNING:
Electricity is dangerous and can kill. Always ask an adult before you use anything electrical.

What is electricity?

You can't see electricity, but you can see what it does. Electricity is made up of tiny particles called electrons. It is used to power computers and even cars. Electricity can be made and it can occur naturally.

We use electricity every day to cook, to turn on the lights, and to keep warm. But electricity is dangerous, so ask an adult before you use anything electrical!

I'm using a lot of energy beating this egg!

You'd never believe it but...

Your great-great-grandparents were the first people to use electricity in their homes. However, it was discovered by the ancient Greeks over 2,000 years ago.

COUNT THE MACHINES

Look around your home and count how many machines have to be plugged into a socket and turned on to work. Find out which room has the most electrical devices. Is it the kitchen?

It's easy with an electric eggbeater.

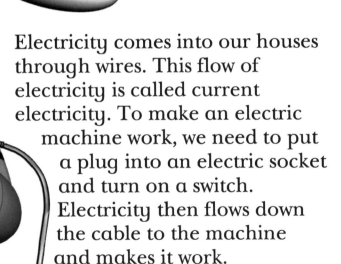

Electricity comes into our houses through wires. This flow of electricity is called current electricity. To make an electric machine work, we need to put a plug into an electric socket and turn on a switch. Electricity then flows down the cable to the machine and makes it work.

Natural electricity

Electricity occurs naturally all around us. Electricity flows through our bodies, carrying messages, while huge bolts of lightning flash in the sky. You can even make another form of natural electricity. It is called static electricity.

Look at the little bits of paper sticking to the balloon.

STICKY BALLOONS

Blow up a balloon and rub it against your hair. What happens to your hair? You have made static electricity that will make the balloon pull things toward itself. Now rub the balloon again and see if the static electricity will make the balloon stick to a wall.

You'd never believe it but...

The middle of a bolt of lightning is hotter than the surface of the sun.

Lightning is a kind of natural electricity. It flashes between the sky and the ground when static electricity builds up in storm clouds. All over the world, there are 6,000 flashes of lightning every minute!

The balloon is making my hair stand on end!

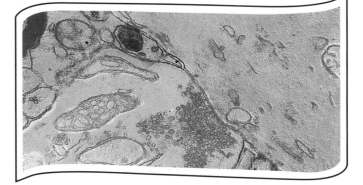

Our bodies pulse with electricity that flows along "cables" called nerves. These carry information between our brain, muscles, and sense organs.

Making electricity

The electricity we use is normally made in power stations. The pressure of steam from boiling water turns a series of blades called turbines very fast. These turbines drive generators, which make the electricity.

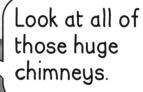

Look at all of those huge chimneys.

You'd never believe it but...

Dead plants can turn on your lights. Coal, oil, and gas come from plants that died millions of years ago. They can all be burned to make electricity.

That's where they burn the fuel to heat the water to make electricity.

TURNING WHEELS
Ride a bicycle for a little while. Can you feel how hard your legs have to work to turn the wheels? The pressure of steam made in the power station does the same job. It turns the blades of the turbines.

Sun, water, wind

Coal-, gas-, and oil-powered stations and nuclear power stations use fuel that will run out one day. So it is important to find other ways of making electricity. Some power stations use water to turn turbines. This is hydroelectric power. Others use the sun and the wind to make electricity.

MAKE A MODEL TURBINE

Put a pencil through the middle of an empty spool. Hold the ends of the pencil, put the spool under the faucet and turn the water on gently. Watch what the water makes the spool do.

The spool is whirling around!

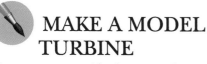

You'd never believe it but...

The sun can be used to make electricity. Huge mirrors are used to focus the sun's heat and make water boil. The steam from this boiling water is then used to turn turbines.

This is similar to how water in a hydroelectric power station makes the turbines spin.

Hey! I'm getting splashed!

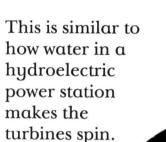

Hydroelectric dams have huge lakes. The pressure of the water flowing through the dam spins turbines.

Each windmill on this farm acts like a turbine. They drive generators to make electricity.

Moving electricity

Current electricity must have a path to travel along to get from one place to another. Electricity can flow through metal, but it cannot flow through plastic. Electricity will travel along a metal wire. The plastic coat around the wire keeps the electricity from escaping, and makes the wire safe.

Electricity is carried from power stations to our homes along very thick cables. These cables are held in the air by tall, metal towers called electric poles.

△ Never touch a bare electric wire. The electricity flowing through it could kill you.

Current electricity is caused by millions of tiny particles called electrons flowing along a wire. One electron bumps into the one in front and pushes it into another electron, and so on, so that they all move along in the same direction.

You'd never believe it but...

Electricity was first used to send messages in a series of beeps known as Morse code.

But I only touched the first one!

You've knocked over all the dominoes!

🖊 KNOCKING OVER DOMINOES

The way electricity flows is similar to the way a row of dominoes will all fall over if one is pushed. Try doing this with a set of dominoes.

Batteries

Batteries contain chemicals that change to make electricity. They are used to power things like a flashlight or a calculator that only need small amounts of electricity. A big machine like a vacuum cleaner would need an enormous battery to make it work for a long time.

My stereo won't work!

It probably needs some new batteries.

When a flashlight is switched on, the chemicals in its batteries change to make electricity and light the bulb. When all of the chemicals in the battery have changed, the battery goes dead and won't work any more. Some special batteries can even be recharged to work again.

LOOKING AT BATTERIES
How many things can you find that use batteries to work? Ask if you can open one of them and take out the batteries. Now see if both ends of the batteries look the same. Does the object work if you put the batteries back the other way?

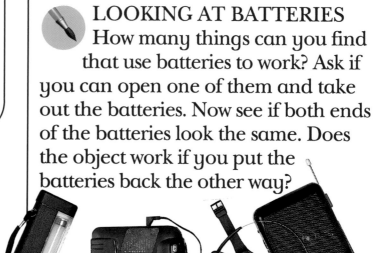

You'd never believe it but...
A lemon can be turned into a battery. Certain metals react with the juice in a lemon to make an electric current.

Switching on and off

Objects that use electricity, such as lights and stereos, have switches that turn them on and off. How many switches can you find at home? But be careful — just look, don't turn any of them on or off!

The light's on!

You'd never believe it but...

Electricity has to travel a great distance from the power station along thick cables before it enters your home. Even so electricity reaches an electrical device the moment you flick on a switch.

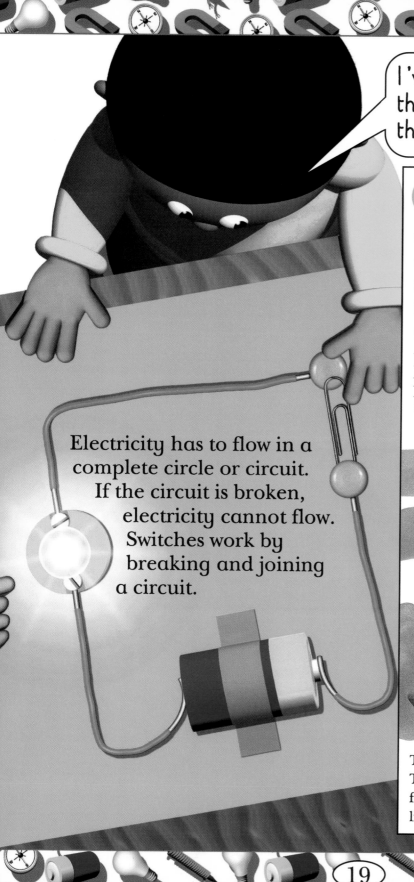

I've moved the paper clip so that the electricity can go all the way around the circuit.

Electricity has to flow in a complete circle or circuit. If the circuit is broken, electricity cannot flow. Switches work by breaking and joining a circuit.

MAKING A CIRCUIT

Ask an adult to help you make a simple circuit like the one below. You will need a small light bulb, some wire, a battery, a metal paper clip, and two thumbtacks. When you move the paper clip away from the tack, the circuit breaks and the light goes off.

This is a very simple circuit. To turn on the light, electricity must flow from the battery, along the wire to the light, then back to the battery again.

Magnetism

Magnets have an invisible force called magnetism. This pulls objects made of iron and steel toward them.

The treasure is seven steps to the south.

USING MAGNETS
If you have a magnet, make a collection of small things and find out which ones the magnet will pick up. Now try putting two magnets together. If they are put a certain way, they will push away from each other.

Magnets have two ends called the north and south poles. A north and a south pole will attract each other. But two of the same poles will try to push each other away.

A compass helps you to find your way. It contains a magnetic needle that can spin inside a box. The needle always points to the north, whichever way the compass is turned.

The compass is pointing to the north.

A long time ago, the Chinese discovered that if they hung a magnet from a thread, one end always pointed to the earth's North Pole and the other to the South Pole. This is how a compass works.

You'd never believe it but...

An ordinary piece of iron or steel will turn into a magnet if it is struck by lightning.

Electromagnets

Electromagnets are used in scrap yards. They are fitted to big cranes and pick up and move objects made of iron and steel.

Ordinary magnets behave like magnets all the time. Electricity can be used to make magnets that can be switched on and off. These are called electromagnets.

My magnet is picking up lots of things.

You'd never believe it but...

Electromagnets are found inside telephones. They help to change electrical signals into sounds that you can hear. Other objects in your home that use electromagnets include washing machines or toy cars with electric motors.

I'm just connecting mine.

 MAKING AN ELECTROMAGNET

Make an electromagnet like the ones that Jack and Jo have made. First, wind some wire around an iron nail as many times as you can. The more times you wind the wire around the nail, the stronger your electromagnet will be. Second, connect the stripped ends of the wire to a battery. Now see what metal objects you can pick up using your homemade electromagnet.

Using electricity

When you go out, look for all the things around you that depend on electricity to work. You might be surprised at how many things are powered by electricity, such as street lights.

Electric traffic lights keep traffic moving safely along.

We're going on an electric train.

You'd never believe it but...

Electricity can power a car. When the car runs low on power, it can be plugged in and recharged.

My toy train uses electricity from a battery.

SAVING ELECTRICITY

Saving electricity can help to burn less coal, oil, and gas in power stations and to keep the air cleaner. Make sure that you shut windows to keep heat in during winter. Turn off faucets to save hot water that uses energy to heat it. Also, turn off all electric appliances that are not being used, such as radios, televisions, and lights.

Life without electricity

Have you ever been in a power blackout when the electricity doesn't work? If you have, then it will help you to imagine what life without electricity would be like.

You'd never believe it but...

Many people in the world live without electricity. They have to cook, clean, and keep warm without power.

I'm bored! I wish the electricity would come on again.

CLEANING THE FLOOR

Today, we take electricity for granted. Try cleaning a carpet with a broom. Now ask an adult if you can use an electric vacuum cleaner. Which gets the job done quicker?

You can read by candlelight.

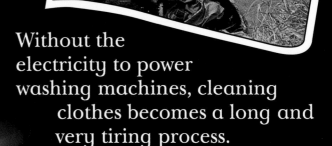

Without the electricity to power washing machines, cleaning clothes becomes a long and very tiring process.

Without electricity, people use candles and oil lamps to light their homes. These lights are not very bright and may not give out a constant light. Wood or coal is burned in stoves or open fires for cooking and keeping warm.

Keeping safe

Electricity is useful to us, but it is also very powerful — you should always follow safety rules when you use it. Batteries are the safest way to learn about electricity, but never cut a battery open because the chemicals inside are dangerous.

Never play with wall sockets or stick things in them. Plastic covers stop babies from putting their fingers in electric sockets.

Pulling a string is a funny way to turn on the light!

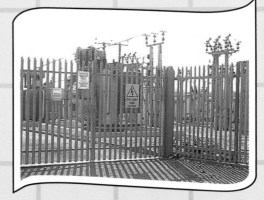

The electricity in overhead cables is very dangerous and can kill anyone who touches one. Never try to climb up electric poles or transformers.

You'd never believe it but...

An electric eel uses electricity as a weapon. It can give an electric shock strong enough to stun a human being!

Lightning can be dangerous. If you are caught outside when there is lightning don't stand under a tree or a tall object.

Electricity flows through water. You should keep all electrical objects away from water. Make sure your hands are dry before you touch anything electrical.

You can't touch a switch with wet hands!

Glossary

Battery

Batteries come in different shapes, but they are usually quite small. Chemicals inside batteries change to make electric currents that can be used to power flashlights, radios, and other things. They are even used to start cars.

Circuit

Current electricity needs to flow around a circle of wire, or circuit. If there is a break in the wire, then the electricity will stop flowing. A switch can open and close a circuit to make electricity flow or stop.

Current electricity

Current electricity is not still; it flows. Current electricity flows from power stations along thick cables to our homes.

Electricity

Electricity is a type of energy that we use to power objects. It is made up of tiny things called electrons that are too small to see.

Electromagnet

An electromagnet is a magnet that can be switched on and off. Wire is coiled around a piece of metal, such as a nail. When electricity is passed along the wire it turns the nail into a magnet.

Electron

An electron is a particle too tiny to see that is charged with electricity. Electrons bump together, pushing each other along the wire to make electricity flow.

Generator

A generator makes electricity when it is turned by a turbine.

Hydroelectric power

This form of power uses the pressure of fast-flowing water to spin turbines very quickly. These turbines then turn generators to make electricity.

Lightning

We see lightning light up the sky as it flashes between the sky and the ground or jumps from cloud to cloud during a thunderstorm. It is a kind of natural electricity formed when static electricity builds up in a thunder cloud.

Magnet

A magnet is usually made of iron or steel. It has an invisible force around it that pulls objects made of iron or steel toward it. A magnet has two ends, one called the north pole, the other called the south pole.

Magnetism

Magnetism is the invisible force around a magnet that pulls metal objects toward it. The same invisible force pushes magnets apart if they are put together with the same poles facing each other.

Power station

Power stations are places where electricity is made. Electricity can be made by burning oil, coal, or gas, by nuclear power, or by the action of water or wind.

Static electricity

Static electricity is a kind of electricity that is still; it does not flow.

Turbine

Turbines have a series of blades that are fixed to a pole. The pressure of water, steam, or gas passing through the blades causes them to spin very quickly.

Index

PHOTO CREDITS

Abbreviations: t-top, m-middle, b-bottom, r-right, l-left, c-center
All the photography in this book is by Roger Vlitos except the following pages: 6 — Mary Evans Picture Library; 9t, 24-25, & 25t both — Frank Spooner Pictures; 9b — Science Photo Library; 10, 13t & b, & 18m — Pictor International; 11, 12, & 29r — Bruce Coleman Collection; 13m, 26, & 27t — Eye Ubiquitous, 14 — AEA Technology; 22 — Spectrum Color Library.